This book is to be returned on or before
the last date stamped below.

Contents

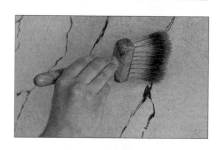

Introduction

This book contains all the information you need to create both simple and more complicated paint effects for every room in your home.

In 'Ideas and Choices' we hope to inspire you with the many different finishes you can create throughout the house on a wide range of surfaces. Much of the equipment necessary is used for standard decorating, but in 'Tools and Materials' we also show those items that are vital for a professional finish and offer some alternatives. For a successful result it is important to plan colour schemes and prepare the surface to be decorated carefully. In 'Planning and Preparation' we give easy-to-follow guidelines.

Paint and water applied with a sponge or rag can create some stunning effects. These easy techniques are covered in 'Simple Paint Effects'. Then you can go on to using longer-drying glazes that allow you time to work on the surface and produce some exciting and unique results. We cover these in 'More Advanced Paint Finishes'.

Distressing techniques produce the softened look of age, as described in 'Antiquing and Illusions', where we also show you how easy it is to use paint to mimic expensive materials.

Even now, after years of using and teaching paint finishes we are constantly coming up with new tips and short-cuts which we are happy to share with you here. Have fun creating paint finishes and effects!

Ideas and Choices

Great flexibility and style can be achieved using paint effects. However, this versatility also makes the choice of style, pattern and colour more difficult, since you have complete control over all three. Here, some inspirational ideas are offered from a selection of rooms or furniture where paint effects have been used. Finishes can be subtle or outrageous, and suited to almost every surface, creating the ideal complement for your home and furniture. Prepare your work with care, allow time to play and experiment with samples, and you will be amazed at the results. But beware, this is a rewarding but addictive pastime, so be prepared to become a paint finish junkie!

Ragged and colour-washed effects

For these paint effects tiny quantities of paint are needed, together with common-place household items such as sponges and rags. The techniques are quick and easy and very economical as well. Very little skill is required, although all finishes should be tested by doing samples before starting your work. Single or multi-coloured washes create hazy, shaded effects, while ragged and rag-rolled treatments create a wonderful marbled look, in which colours are easily co-ordinated to blend with your furnishings.

▶ Blue colour washing creates a sea and sky effect that is perfect for bathrooms.

▶ A wild, multi-coloured wash is ideal in this ultra-modern bedroom for a teenager. Colour washing the radiator makes it blend in with the walls.

▼ A distinctive colour wash in warm, earthy shades gives the impression of age to bare plaster and provides a great backdrop to this modern sculpture.

◀ Pale cherry wash applied in vertical strokes creates an informal but stylish look, ideal for a sitting room.

▼ This subtle rag rolling in two colours blends perfectly with a fawn background, creating just the right mood with just the right shades.

▶ Ragged walls can easily co-ordinate with your furnishings, as colours can be mixed to match exactly.

◀ Ragging in two colours over white-painted walls helps to break up large expanses with a marble-like texture.

Effects with bags and brushes

Water- or oil-based glazes can be blended or worked together, or partially removed from the surface. Improvised tools, from a plastic bag to a toothbrush, may be used to create unique textures. Dragging forms a perfect frame to enhance other finishes such as stippling or colour washing, while multi-coloured bagging will amaze you with its ease and beauty. If a wall seems a big project, build up your confidence and experiment on a smaller surface such as a door or a piece of furniture first.

▼ A highlighting line is rubbed into the mouldings of these fitted cupboards, contrasting well with the otherwise subtle stippling and dragging.

▲ This mirror frame and wardrobe are subtly dragged and stippled in a lemon yellow glaze over a white background to create a clean, fresh look.

▲ Bagging produces a wonderful texture on these doors, rich yet still subtle.

◀ Pink and green complement each other and are blended together using stippling on this wardrobe.

▲ Tongue-and-groove boarding looks good dragged to highlight its verticality. The toilet seat was colour washed and then varnished.

▲ This headboard is dragged and bagged to provide a suitable background for the stencilled image and to blend with the treatment of the wall.

Marble finishes

Paint effects which imitate stone and marble are always popular. Glazes allow time to blend colours, and their transparent quality resembles that of the surfaces you are imitating. This sort of work takes time, so prepare with care, and use a photograph or sample to provide a realistic original to copy. Large areas can be broken down into smaller ones, which look realistic and are easier to work with. Stone blocks can be created using masking tape or a stencil. Experiment with veining techniques using feathers, brushes or even a piece of old card.

▼ Veining, which was created by using both rag and brush, gives a cool, marble-like effect.

▲ This marbled cornice (shown in detail, right) and skirting provide an interesting frame to the patterned walls, and the different textures compete well.

◄ Colours are beautifully mixed and blended to co-ordinate well with the walls.

◀ Two contrasting marbles can be used together to great effect, enhanced by the dark colouring of the dado rail and skirting.

▼ This bagged, fantasy marble, bold and dark and finished with a gloss varnish, is ideally suited to the area below the dado.

◀ An original, but damaged slate fireplace has marbled panels to blend in.

▲ Stone effects are well suited to stairs. Contrasting treatments look less austere.

A variety of finishes

Paint effects can be used in all sorts of situations to create the illusion of age, disguise a poor surface, or simply create a great look. Wood graining can be used on any surface for naturalistic or fantasy effects, while crackle finishes can create an impression of age on smaller items such as boxes or picture frames. You can transform an uninteresting piece of furniture into a prized possession with a paint finish, and once the base coat is painted all the hard work is done.

▲ The combination of light sponging above a dado and bolder rag rolling below is ideal in many situations.

▼ Two colours are stippled together on these panelled doors and the effect enhanced with lining round the moulding.

◄ This new pine display case is treated with a waxed distressed finish, using blue emulsion over a white emulsion base.

▼ The mouldings and edges of these cupboards are highlighted using a distressing technique.

▲ Colour-washed timber is very effective, and better than stained varnish which tends to hide the grain.

Tools and Materials

Although all sorts of very effective paint finishes can be produced using standard decorating paints and tools, in some cases special tools and materials will produce the finest results. In a very few cases there is no alternative to using either a special solution or a professional tool.

Basic tools

Most people who have carried out any home decorating will be familiar with, and probably already have, most of the tools covered in this section. It generally pays to buy tools and equipment of the best quality – well looked after, they will last for years. Keep a supply of small items such as sandpaper and steel wool, card and rags so that you have them to hand when the decorating mood takes you.

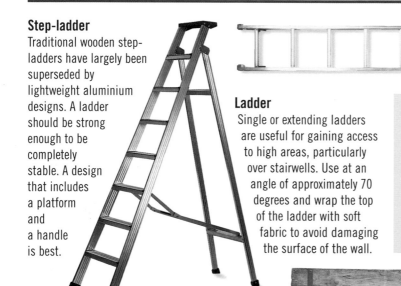

Step-ladder
Traditional wooden step-ladders have largely been superseded by lightweight aluminium designs. A ladder should be strong enough to be completely stable. A design that includes a platform and a handle is best.

Ladder
Single or extending ladders are useful for gaining access to high areas, particularly over stairwells. Use at an angle of approximately 70 degrees and wrap the top of the ladder with soft fabric to avoid damaging the surface of the wall.

SAFETY NOTE
Make sure that a step-ladder or ladder is secure and on an even surface before mounting it. Adjust if necessary.

Scaffold board
Placed over the rungs of equally matched step-ladders, one at each end, provides a platform when working on high areas.

Dust sheets
Decorators' dust sheets or old bed sheets protect furniture and floors and absorb spills.

Standard decorators' paintbrushes
A range of good quality decorators' brushes is essential for basic painting. Brushes that are well looked after improve with age.

Short-haired roller
Applies oil or acrylic glazes to large flat surfaces fast.

Sand-, abrasive or glass paper
Use medium to fine paper during preparation and between coats of varnish.

Spirit level
Ensures that horizontal and vertical lines are accurate.

Steel rule
Measures distances for preparing large areas of marbling.

Chalked plumb line
Creates a vertical chalk mark for use as a guideline for rag rolling. Alternatively use a large key attached to chalk-coated string.

Masking tape
Protects adjoining areas when working.

Tape measure and chalk
For accurate measuring and marking of your work before starting and drawing outlines and marking joints between marbled slabs.

Steel wool
Medium- to fine-grade steel wool is used for distressing and applying wax to timber.

Old cotton towel
Removes glazes from brushes and other applicators.

Screw-top glass jars with rubber seals
For mixing paint solutions; must be leak-proof when shaken.

Rags
For ragging use well-washed polyester and cotton mixture fabric cut into approximately 30cm (12in) squares or slightly larger.

Stiff card
A piece of stiff card approximately 30cm by 20cm (12in by 8in) acts as a guard to protect adjoining surfaces when applying most simple paint finishes.

Old plate
Useful for mopping up small quantities of paint solution when sponging or colour washing.

Open top tubs
Hold paint or glaze when ragging or rag rolling and allow rag to be re-wetted easily.

Specialist tools

Although in many cases you can use an alternative that will produce a good result at a fraction of the cost, there is no real substitute for the specialist brushes used for specific paint finish techniques. Buy the best brushes you can afford and look after them by cleaning immediately after use with a proprietary cleaner or soapy water (depending on the type of paint used) and hanging them up to dry.

Flogger
Use large flogging brushes for large areas of dragging, simple graining or colour washing.

Distemper brush
Can be used as an alternative to a flogger.

Mixed bristle dragging brush
Produces a variety of lined effects. An ordinary long-bristled decorators' brush or a dust brush can also be used.

Wallpaper brush
Can be used as an alternative to a dragger or a flogger for washes.

Softening brushes
Blend and soften many finishes. Badger hair is the softest but as many badgers are killed each year to produce these brushes, they are best avoided. Instead keep a dragging or a soft dust brush for this purpose.

Hog-hair softening brush

Badger-hair softening brush

Small dragging brush
Useful for detail work, such as the frame of a panelled door.

Dust brush
An alternative to a flogger or a dragging brush. Also used with softening brushes.

Stippling brushes
Available in a wide range of sizes and used frequently for glaze finishes. Alternatively use plastic or rubber textured plaster brushes or nylon block brushes (rubber perishes after a while when used with oil glaze).

Nylon block brush
An economical alternative to a traditional stippling brush.

Alternative stippling brushes
Plastic or rubber textured plaster brushes can also be used.

Sea sponge
Should have a good texture on both faces and ideally be unbleached. Choose one to fit your hand size – about 12cm (5in) in diameter.

Synthetic sponge
A cotton or synthetic sponge can be used but may require shaping with scissors.

Rubber squeegee
Used for rubbing off a dark coloured glaze from the raised relief parts of a textured surface to expose a lighter coloured base.

Combs
Made of metal or rubber these are ideal for wood graining and other combed finishes.

Rockers
For producing a realistic open heartwood grain with either oil- or water-based glazes.

Feathers or fine artists' brush
Applies fine veins when marbling. The artists' brush can also be used for touching up details in any fine work.

USING FEATHERS
Goose feathers are said to be best for painting in veining. This is done as a final stage in creating realistic or fantasy marbling. Alternatively, dipping a feather in solvent and lightly working it over the coloured glaze removes a little of the glaze and blurs the edges to reproduce a softly veined effect.

Plastic carrier bags
Use to apply paint when bagging or marbling.

Bunch of keys
Beaten against a wooden surface imitates knocks and bruises of age.

Brass-bristled brush
Removes soft grain from wooden surfaces prior to liming.

Paints and materials

Most paint finishes use large quantities of water mixed with small quantities of strong-colour water-based paint or water-based glazes, or, alternatively, oil-based paints and oil scumble glaze. A few special effects require the special solutions, listed here. For creating paint effects, a few standard decorating materials are also extremely useful.

Eggshell and satin finish oil-based paint
For hard-wear areas and ideal as a base for glaze finishes.

Emulsion paint
Suitable for general decorating, this water-based paint can also be diluted for simple paint effects.

Stencil paint
Strong colour choices make this quick-drying water-based paint ideal for simple paint effects or for tinting acrylic glazes.

Acrylic paint
Plastic, tough and resilient and also water-based, this is suitable for tinting acrylic scumble glaze.

Artists' oils
Strong pigment spirit-based paint ideal for tinting oil-based scumble glaze.

Artists' acrylic
Strong pigment water-based paint ideal for tinting acrylic scumble glaze.

Universal stainers
Strong pigmented colour tints for paint or glaze.

CAUTION

Paints and glazes containing solvents may cause irritation to the skin and therefore gloves should be worn.

Acrylic scumble glaze

A water-based medium which may be tinted and used as an alternative to oil glaze. It is unaffected by sun or heat but has a relatively short working time.

Oil scumble glaze

Transparent oil-based medium for use as transparent oil glaze. This can be tinted to suit your own colour choices and has a long working time but yellows on exposure to sun and heat.

Gilt cream

Beeswax and turpentine wax with metal powder, used as a highlighter or to repair gilt surfaces.

Liming wax

Mixture of beeswax and titanium white powder used to lime open grain timber.

Turpentine-based clear wax polish

Protects finishes on painted or wooden furniture and used to distress water-based emulsion paint.

Wax candle

Used to simulate areas of high wear when creating distressed effects. Wax is rubbed on selected areas only.

Petroleum jelly

Thick oil medium which does not set. Used in distressing timber.

WHITE SPIRIT

A solvent for oil-based paints and glazes. It is also an economical alternative to pure turpentine. White spirit is used for diluting oil-based paints and glazes to the required consistency. Most equipment used for applying oil-based solutions should be cleaned thoroughly using white spirit.

PAINTS AND MATERIALS CONTINUED

Acrylic crackle glaze
Splits and crazes two layers of emulsion or acrylic paint, as shown below.

Acrylic crackle varnish
Produces surface cracks similar to those found in old varnish.

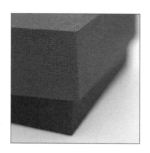

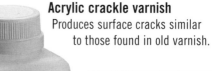

Patina varnish
Oil-based varnish that is used with gum arabic — also known as cracking varnish — to produce craquelure, or fine cracking similar to that on old porcelain or oil paintings.

Gum arabic
Used with patina varnish to produce craquelure (see left). Craquelure creates a more delicate crazed effect than acrylic crackle glaze or acrylic crackle varnish, shown in the detail, right.

Varnishes
Can be acrylic or oil-based and either sprayed or applied with a brush to protect the finish.

Emulsion glaze
Water-based protective medium, similar to varnish, which dries to a clear matt finish.

▲ **Acrylic varnish**

► **Oil-based varnish**

▲ **Spray varnish**

TERABINE
A medium which reduces the drying time when mixed with oil-based paints and glazes.

PAINT MATERIALS AND THEIR USES

MATERIAL	SOLVENT	USE	ADVANTAGE	DISADVANTAGE	HAZARD
EMULSION	Water	General decorating Dilute for simple paint effects	Cheap and huge range of colours Quick drying	Not resistant to heavy wear	Minimal
ACRYLIC	Water	General decorating For small items	Reasonable colour range and durable Quick drying	Not widely available and relatively expensive	Minimal
EGGSHELL	White spirit	General decorating For all surfaces	Widely available Good colour range and durable	Relatively expensive Slow to dry	Avoid prolonged contact Unpleasant smell
TRANSPARENT OIL SCUMBLE	White spirit	Suitable for use tinted for decorative glaze finishes	Long working time Nice to use	Tends to yellow Long drying time	Avoid prolonged contact Unpleasant smell
ACRYLIC SCUMBLE	Water	Suitable for use tinted for decorative glaze finishes	Quick drying time No yellowing	Short working time	Minimal but smell can be unpleasant
STENCIL PAINT	Water	Use as base paint or as tint for acrylic glaze	Good colour range Quick drying	Not widely available	Minimal
ARTISTS' OILS	White spirit	Use to tint oil glaze	Good colour range Widely available Concentrated pigments	Expensive Can reduce drying time	Pigments can be toxic
UNIVERSAL STAINERS	White spirit	Use to tint oil glaze	Widely available	Poor colour range	Pigments can be toxic
ACRYLIC VARNISH	Water	Protective medium used over water-based paints	No discolouration Quick drying	May cause staining over oil bases	Minimal
OIL VARNISH	White spirit	Protective medium For any surface	Very durable Widely available	Slow drying Tends to yellow	Avoid prolonged contact Smell can be unpleasant
EMULSION GLAZE	Water	Protective medium	Quick drying Completely clear	Not very durable	Minimal
PATINA VARNISH	White spirit	Ageing surfaces and craquelure	Ideal for authentic look	Expensive	Avoid prolonged contact
GUM ARABIC	Water	Used with patina varnish to produce craquelure	Ideal for authentic look	Expensive Can be re-softened Requires protection	Avoid prolonged contact
ACRYLIC CRACKLE GLAZE	Water	Produces rough splitting of two water-based paints	Rapid and effective process, but needs care	Difficult to apply Limited-size surfaces only	Minimal
ACRYLIC CRACKLE VARNISH	Water	Produces random cracking on water-based paints	Rapid and effective process, but needs care	Difficult to apply Limited-size surfaces only	Minimal
WAX	Turpentine	Wax finishing and distressing	Good finish	Needs regular re-application	Avoid prolonged contact

Planning and Preparation

Before applying any paint finish it is important to plan the colour scheme carefully. Select colours to co-ordinate with objects in the room and to suit the room's shape and aspect, then create a number of alternative colour samples. Fix these to wall, floor or whatever surface is to be decorated and look at them in both daylight and artificial light, alongside other furnishings. Then make your choice.

It is also vital that the surface to be decorated is prepared correctly, bearing in mind the particular paint finish that is to be applied. Some effects hide a bad surface, others highlight it; the chart (see pages 36–37) gives you more information.

This chapter contains

Choosing colours

A basic understanding of how colours can be mixed, and how they interact is essential. However, the best way to ensure successful results for a scheme is to prepare a number of colour samples and display them for a few days in the room to be decorated. Often the first choice will be superseded by a less obvious one.

MIXING COLOURS

In theory all colours can be created from the three primaries, blue, yellow and red, together with black and white. The example (right), which blends together three glazes mixed with primary bases (see pages 52–55), illustrates how the primary colours blend and how difficult it is to achieve colours with true vibrance and purity. But manufacturers now produce such vast colour ranges that mixing can be limited to adjusting ready-mixed colours.

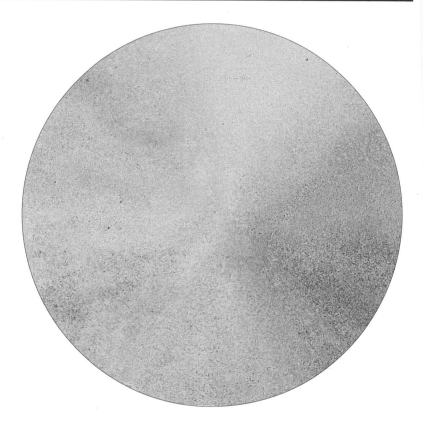

Using the colour wheel

When combining colours for colour schemes these are three simple rules to follow to ensure successful results.

Complementary colours

Colours on opposite sides of the colour wheel are known as complementary colours because together they create a full complement of all the spectral hues. Each is the other's strongest possible contrast, showing it up most vividly, as when oranges are wrapped in blue or purple tissue, or butchers decorate a window display with green leaves.

Closely related colours

Colours that appear next to each other on the colour wheel are closely related and always blend well with one another. However, a scheme made up only of closely-related colours lacks the zing that contrasts introduce.

Harmonizing colours

Three colours equidistant on the colour wheel will harmonize with each other.

Reducing colour strength

When two complementary colours are mixed they produce a grey midtone. This can be usefully exploited when mixing colours. If a colour is too vibrant the addition of its complementary colour produces a less vibrant, but still clean, colour. White reduces colour strength to produce a tint while retaining its purity.

Colour clarity is impaired by adding black

Colour value is reduced and made lighter by adding white

Creating a balanced scheme

The intensity of a colour is a measure of how dull or vivid it is, while its value measures how dark or light it is. A balanced scheme is one in which no one colour used overpowers the others. It is as important to use colours of similar intensity and value as it is to co-ordinate them.

Mixed complementary colours produce grey midtones

THE EFFECT OF LIGHT ON COLOUR

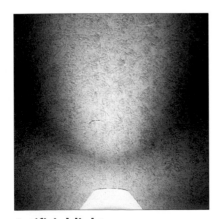

Artificial light

Light affects the appearance of colours. In yellowish artificial light, blue may seem green.

Natural daylight

It is important to check colours you intend to use in both natural daylight and artificial light.

COLOUR COMBINATIONS

To devise successful colour schemes, take note of the colours used in a room that particularly appeals to you and also look at how colour combinations work in nature. Always remember that a room's decorations should act as a backdrop to your treasured possessions rather than overpower them.

Using colour cleverly

Choice of the right colour scheme can considerably enhance a room, changing both its atmosphere and its apparent shape. Is the room light or dark, sunny or cold? Is it long and thin, or perhaps small yet high-ceilinged? What is its use? Take all these considerations into account when making colour choices, for choices based on improving aspect as well as simply on colour preference determine the success or failure of a scheme. Success can be achieved by chance but it is much better to depend on careful planning.

CHOOSING THE STYLE

It is the flexibility and ease with which you can choose colours, styles and textures that gives paint finishes an advantage over other forms of decorating. But this very flexibility can be a source of bewilderment and make it hard to know where to begin.

As a start, some key decorators' principles are illustrated in the drawings on this and the opposite page. These show the effect of colours that are dark and light, warm and cold, and also how patterns of

different kinds can affect the apparent shape and size of a room.

The first stage of planning a scheme for decorating a whole room – before you begin to test out colour samples as described on page 28 – can be done on paper. Take a photograph of the room you intend to decorate, then make several photocopies. Colouring in the photocopies in your possible schemes will soon show up any problems and help you to decide which works well.

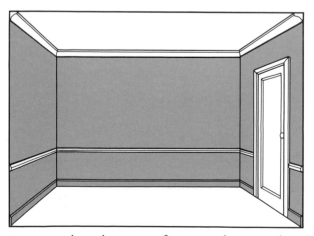

A warm colour draws a surface towards you and can create a cosy effect.

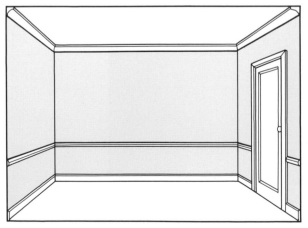

A cool colour takes the surface away from you and creates an impression of space.

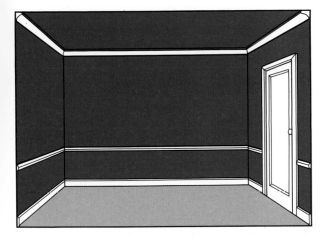

A dark colour also draws a surface towards you and can make the ceiling appear lower.

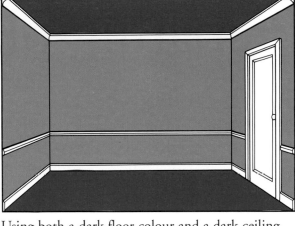

Using both a dark floor colour and a dark ceiling colour draws the two surfaces together.

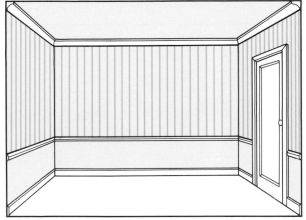

Vertical stripes draw the eye upwards and therefore appear to heighten a room.

Large patterns bring walls towards you and can make a room appear claustrophobic.

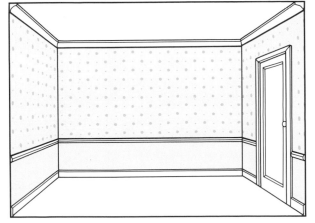

Small patterns, like cool colours, create an illusion of space.

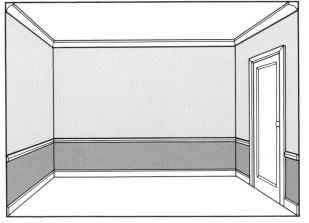

Darker colour on the lower walls encloses the space; a light area above creates an illusion of space.

Preparing plaster surfaces

The key to a successful result is preparing the surfaces to be decorated correctly. Not all surfaces need to be perfect, but they must be appropriate for the finish you want. Check the smoothness of a wall finish by rubbing your hand over it. A rough or textured surface cannot be dragged, but can be sponged or ragged successfully. The surface preparation chart (see pages 36–37) gives suggestions for the ideal surface for each paint finish. Consult a book specializing in home decorating for a more detailed guide to preparing surfaces.

PLASTER SURFACES

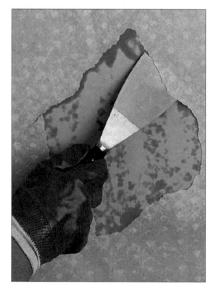  

1 First use a scraper to remove wallpaper, or loose and flaky paint and plaster, then lightly sand the surface. Protect your hands with gloves and wear a mask while working to ensure that you do not inhale dust.

2 Clean down the surface with a solution of liquid detergent or sugar soap. Use a proprietary filler to make good any holes, filling them slightly proud of the surface, to allow for shrinkage to occur when dry.

3 Sand back when the filler has dried. Between wood and walls use a flexible filler to make good the joints and remove excess filler with a sponge.

4 Apply the base-coat paint, using a brush, roller or pad. At least two coats will be required. Lightly sand the surface between coats. Always follow the manufacturer's instructions and take note of any hazard warnings.

PROBLEMS AND SOLUTIONS

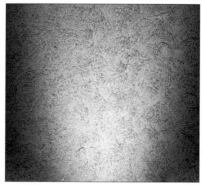

Disguising poor surfaces

Rag rolling in two colours (see pages 46–47) is not only quick, economical and easy but is also a good finish for disguising a poor or uneven surface.

Careful lighting

Remember that lighting that casts a pool of light across a wall draws attention to any imperfections. Avoid highlighting surfaces you know are poor, even if you have used a paint finish to help to disguise them.

Heavy-weight papers

Beware when removing wood-chip or anaglypta papers. They are difficult to remove, and a poor surface beneath may start to disintegrate when you try. Heavy sponging, using two or more colours (see pages 42–43), can help to disguise these textured surfaces of this type.

CAUTION

Always observe the manufacturer's instructions, particularly when using any substances containing solvents.

HORSEHAIR AND LIME PLASTER

Delicate old plaster surfaces may need repair. Use bonding plaster with a small amount of PVA bonding agent for extra strength.

Preparing wood surfaces

Timber furniture and fittings lend themselves to the use of glaze finishes (see pages 52–73) or to antiquing and illusions (see pages 74–91). However, thorough preparation is required to produce a good end result. All modern wooden surfaces, from medium density fibreboard (MDF) to melamine-finished chipboard, can be painted ready for the appropriate finish to be applied. Consult a specialist home decorating book for more detailed information. The finish guide (see pages 36–37) lists the base coats required beneath the different paint finishes dealt with in this book.

WOOD AND WOOD SUBSTITUTE SURFACES

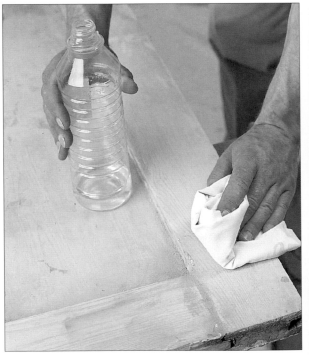

1 Prepare surfaces by lightly sanding to smooth rough edges and to provide a key for the paint. On painted surfaces or melamine, clean down first, using a detergent solution or sugar soap. Then follow the instructions in step 2 before applying further paint.

2 Remove all dust, first with a dust brush and then with a lint-free rag dampened with white spirit. Seal knots with shellac or knotting. A tack rag, available from decorators' merchants, removes dust from surfaces to leave an ideal clean surface to work on.

3 Most paints are best applied in several thin coats. Before painting, coat a bare timber surface with both primer and undercoat.

4 Smooth the surface with fine-grade sandpaper before starting and between coats. Traditionally, furniture and fitments such as kitchen, bedroom and bathroom cupboards are painted with oil-based paints as these paints are considered more durable.

5 When applying paint finishes, use the most appropriate base for the particular finish (see pages 36–37). A final coat of varnish can be used to protect either a water-based or oil-based paint finish from hard wear.

USING MDF

Although most traditional softwoods and hardwoods provide excellent surfaces for paint finishes, modern MDF is the ideal surface. Take care when preparing an MDF surface, as the dust produced on sanding is toxic. Wear a mask and work outside if possible or, if not, in a well-ventilated area.

CAUTION

Always observe the manufacturer's instructions, particularly when using any substances containing solvents.

CHOOSING PAINTS

FINISH	SPONGING	RAGGING – ON	RAG ROLLING – ON	COLOUR WASHING – SIMPLE	DRAGGING	RAG ROLLING – OFF	STIPPLING	BAGGING	COLOUR WASHING – ADVANCED
PAGE REF	42	44	46	48	56	58	60	64	68
TECHNIQUE 1–10 Easy – Hard	1	1	2	2	2	3	2	2	3
IDEAL BASE	Matt emulsion	Matt emulsion	Matt emulsion	Matt emulsion	Eggshell paint	Eggshell paint	Eggshell paint	Eggshell paint	Eggshell paint
OTHER SUITABLE BASES	Silk emulsion	Silk emulsion	Silk emulsion	Silk emulsion	Vinyl silk emulsion Varnish Melamine	Vinyl silk emulsion Varnish Melamine	Vinyl silk emulsion Varnish Melamine	Vinyl silk emulsion Varnish Melamine	Vinyl silk emulsion Varnish Melamine
BASE SURFACE	Possible on rough/poor surfaces	Possible on rough/poor surfaces	Possible on rough/poor surfaces	Possible on rough/poor surfaces	Good and smooth surface required	Any surface	Any surface	Any surface	Highlights imperfections
PAINT FINISH MEDIUM	Water-based paint solutions	Water-based paint solutions	Water-based paint solutions	Water-based paint solutions	Oil or acrylic scumble glaze	Oil or acrylic scumble glaze	Oil or acrylic scumble glaze	Oil or acrylic scumble glaze	Oil or acrylic scumble glaze
PROTECTION RECOM- MENDED	None	None	None	None	Suitable varnish	Suitable varnish	Suitable varnish	Suitable varnish	Suitable varnish
SUITABLE SURFACES	Walls or furniture	Walls or furniture	Walls or furniture	Walls or furniture	Walls or furniture	Walls or furniture	Walls or furniture	Walls or furniture	Walls or furniture
TOXICITY AND HAZARDS	Safe	Safe	Safe	Safe	Avoid prolonged skin contact with oil glaze and dispose of waste safely	Avoid prolonged skin contact with oil glaze and dispose of waste safely	Avoid prolonged skin contact with oil glaze and dispose of waste safely	Avoid prolonged skin contact with oil glaze and dispose of waste safely	Avoid prolonged skin contact with oil glaze and dispose of waste safely

COLOUR RUBBING	COMBING	DISTRESSING	WAX AGEING	ACRYLIC CRACKLE	CRAQUELURE	LIMING	MARBLING	WOOD GRAINING – COMBS	WOOD GRAINING – ROCKERS
70	72	76	78	80	82	84	86	90	90
2	3	4	3	7	6	3	8	7	5
Eggshell paint	Eggshell paint	Any	Vinyl matt emulsion	Vinyl emulsion or acrylic paint	Eggshell paint	Open-grain timber	Eggshell paint	Eggshell paint	Eggshell paint
Vinyl silk emulsion Varnish Melamine	Vinyl silk emulsion Varnish Melamine	None	None	None	Any sealed surface	None	Vinyl silk emulsion Varnish Melamine	Vinyl silk emulsion Varnish Melamine	Vinyl silk emulsion Varnish Melamine
Highlights imperfections	Good surface required	Highlights imperfections	Highlights imperfections	Highlights imperfections	Any surface	Any surface	Good surface required	Good surface required	Good surface required
Oil or acrylic scumble glaze	Oil or acrylic scumble glaze	Petroleum jelly or wax	Turpentine based furniture wax	Acrylic crackle glaze/ varnish	Patina varnish and gum arabic	Liming wax	Oil or acrylic scumble glaze	Oil or acrylic scumble glaze	Oil or acrylic scumble glaze
Suitable varnish	Suitable varnish	Suitable varnish	None	Varnish	Oil-based varnish	Furniture wax	Suitable varnish	Suitable varnish	Suitable varnish
Textured surfaces	Walls or furniture	Furniture	Furniture or wood panelling	Small simple furniture	Any surface, small is best	Any open-grain timber	Walls or furniture	Walls or furniture	Walls or furniture
Avoid prolonged skin contact with oil glaze and dispose of waste safely	Avoid prolonged skin contact with oil glaze and dispose of waste safely	Avoid prolonged skin contact with turpentine base waxes	Avoid prolonged skin contact with turpentine base waxes	Safe	Avoid prolonged contact with patina varnish	Avoid prolonged contact with wax containing turpentine and titanium	Avoid prolonged skin contact with oil glaze and dispose of waste safely	Avoid prolonged skin contact with oil glaze and dispose of waste safely	Avoid prolonged skin contact with oil glaze and dispose of waste safely

Simple Paint Effects

For flexibility, style, speed and affordability, it is difficult to beat these simple paint effects. Some are traditional, adapted from more complicated glaze finishes (see pages 52–73), while some are new effects which have been made possible by the paints now available. You will be amazed at how easy it is to master something that can provide the ideal decorating medium, and give you total control over both colour and pattern. This means that the finish you create will be individual to you. Once you have completed one effect, you will want to go on to use many more of them.

This chapter contains

Mixing colours

All paint effects can be made easy by careful planning and preparation. Always do a sample first to perfect the technique and style, and check the chosen colour scheme in both natural and artificial light. Paint solutions use surprisingly small quantities of strong-colour paint, mixed with surprisingly large volumes of water to give cheap but stunning results. A small glass jar containing just 15ml (1 tbsp) of paint and half filled with water should be sufficient to sponge two medium-size rooms.

MATERIALS: Strong-colour water-based paint (stencil, emulsion or acrylic paint), screw-top glass jar with a rubber seal, measuring jug, absorbent towel or cloth

TYPICAL DILUTIONS AND COVERAGE FOR WATER–BASED FINISHES

	WATER : PAINT*	COVERAGE
SPONGING	10/30 : 1	3ml per sq metre
	(strong/pale)	(less than ½tsp per sq yard)
RAGGING OR RAG ROLLING	5/25 : 1	5ml per sq metre
	(strong/pale)	(1tsp per sq yard)
COLOUR WASHING	10/20 : 1	15ml per sq metre
	(strong/pale)	(1tbsp per sq yard)

*Stencil paint or strongly coloured emulsion

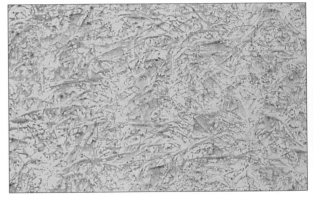

For strong colours use a 5/10 : 1 dilution

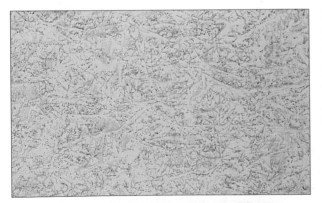

For medium colours use a 20 : 1 dilution

For weak colours use a 30 : 1 dilution

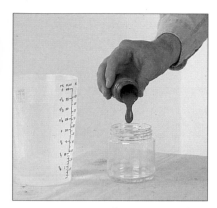

1 Prepare a working area with all your required materials. Pour a small quantity of paint into the screw-top jar.

2 Use a jug to add warm water to the paint in the right proportions to create the effect you want (see chart opposite).

3 Secure the jar top, cover with an absorbent towel or cloth and shake well.

4 Check the base of the jar to ensure the paint is well mixed, otherwise the colour can change during use. Shake again if this is necessary. Prepare a small sample of your chosen finish on lining paper. This allows you to check both finish and colour *in situ* before you start on the surface to be decorated.

DECORATORS' TIPS
Warm water helps to disperse the paint more quickly.

It is important to use the same intensity of all colours when using two or three different colours together.

Once mixed, the paint and water solution should last almost indefinitely provided it is protected from frost.

Sponging

Sponging is one of the quickest and cheapest ways to decorate and co-ordinate a room scheme. It is great fun to apply on walls, furniture or accessories and, depending on the colours you use and the way you apply the sponge, it can provide a backdrop that is soft and subtle or bold and outrageous. It also helps to hide blemishes on the wall surface, even disguising poor plaster or unpopular textured paper (see page 33). Mistakes are easily obliterated: simply sponge on a little undiluted base paint, using a clean sponge.

TOOLS: Natural sea sponge, strip of card

MATERIALS: Dust sheet, paint solutions in 2 or 3 colours, old plate, absorbent towel or cloth

BASE: Water-based emulsion on walls

1 Pour out 15ml (1 tbsp) of paint solution (see pages 40–41) and mop up with the sponge so that it is evenly distributed through the surface.

2 Test on spare paper. Apply sponge to wall in a gentle patting motion, rotating your hand and the sponge as you go, to achieve an even but random build-up of colour.

3 To sponge close to the ceiling or into corners use the strip of stiff but thin card as a shield against the adjacent wall to protect it. Use the cloth to wipe up spills.

4 A paint-loaded sponge covers 6–12sq m (7–14sq yds) before it requires re-loading. For a dense effect, go round the room a few times gradually building up the colour.

5 More colour can always be added but it is more time consuming to remove colour. Check the finish regularly by standing back to look at the effect you are creating. Stop when you have achieved the desired look.

6 Subsequent colours can be added immediately, as the paint dries on the wall within one minute. The same sponge can be used for all colours but must be well washed and dried between colour changes.

7 To harmonize with other items in the room, pick colours which already appear in the room scheme. In this case green is used for the first coat, followed by pink and peach.

DENSITY OF SPONGING

Dense sponging
This produces a bold effect, with shapes blending into an overall pattern.

Light sponging
With lots of spaces showing the base colour, this produces a soft, airy finish.

PREPARE YOURSELF
Always prepare samples before you start on the surface to be decorated. The ideal natural sea sponge should be comfortable to hold and provide an open texture on both the front and back face.

Dry sponges expand when wet, so choose one that is slightly smaller than hand-size when dry – this should fit neatly into your hand when dampened.

A synthetic sponge can be used but does not produce such an interesting pattern.

Ragging

Ragging on, with a water-based paint solution, is a simple variation on traditional ragging. You can choose between a strong, dramatic effect or a soft and subtle look that has a texture similar to crushed velvet. Prepare samples to check the colours and finish before you start work on the surface.

TOOLS: Clean, pre-washed polyester and cotton mix (or pure cotton) rags, without hems, about 30cm (12in) square, strip of thin card

MATERIALS: Dust sheet, water-based paint solutions in 1–3 colours, open-top tub, absorbent cloth

BASE: On walls rag over a base coat of water-based paint such as emulsion

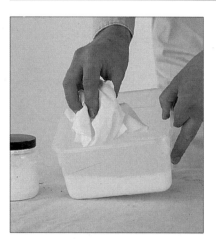

1 On a protected working area, transfer the paint solution (see page 40–41) into an open-topped container. Take the first rag and immerse it in the paint solution.

2 Squeeze out the rag over the tub, catching any drips on the tub edge with the outside of your hand. Any excess paint on your hands will be absorbed by the fabric.

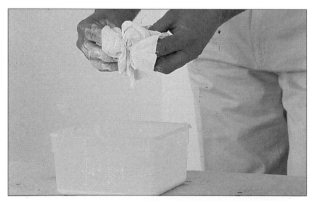

3 Scrunch the rag into a controllable ball. Don't fold it as this results in hard lines appearing in the finished ragging.

4 Apply the rag to the wall using a gentle, patting action, building up the colour in a random pattern until the desired density is achieved.

5 At the corners and tops of walls, use the card to shield the adjacent wall from smudges of paint. Apply the rag close to the corner. Repeat when you start on the next wall.

RE-WETTING THE RAG

After covering about 1sq m (1sq yd), the rag will start to dry out. Refresh it by dipping your hand into the paint solution and wiping it over the rag. Do this twice.

6 Add a second colour on a clean rag, using the same procedure. You can follow this with a further two to three colours, either added at the same time, or applied at a later date.

7 To correct a mistake, sponge on undiluted base paint. If this also obliterates some of the ragging re-do the ragging where it has been lost.

SUBTLE FINISHES

Ragging looks very effective combined with sponging (see pages 42–43) or with colour washing (see pages 48–49).

Light ragging
Light ragging in blue and brown on a dove-grey background.

Blue and brown ragging
Both colours applied on a mid-green background.

USE BARE HANDS

Don't try wearing rubber gloves for ragging, as they are clumsy and can spoil the effect.

STORING SURPLUS PAINT

After use, store the rag in the jar with the remaining solution. It is then readily available if a repair is necessary at a later date.

Rag rolling on

Rag rolling on, using a water-based paint solution, is an easier alternative to the traditional rag rolling off with glazes (see pages 58–59), which is more time consuming and certainly a lot messier. A wonderful 'crinkled' pattern is produced that, like sponging and ragging, hides a poor surface.

TOOLS: Clean, pre-washed polyester and cotton mix (or pure cotton) rags, without hems, about 30cm (12in) square, plumb line, strip of thin card

MATERIALS: Dust sheet, water-based paint solutions in 1–3 colours, open-top tub, absorbent cloth

BASE: On walls rag roll over a base coat of water-based emulsion paint

1 Pour the paint solution (see pages 40–41) into the container, on a protected work surface, and immerse a rag in it.

2 Squeeze out the rag over the tub, wiping the outside of your hand on the edge of the tub to catch drips. Any excess paint on the hands will be absorbed by the fabric.

3 Scrunch the rag into a sausage shape – it must not be folded or rolled neatly. Each time the rag is refreshed with paint, it will need to be re-arranged to avoid creating a repetitive pattern.

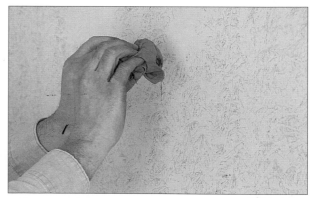

4 Use both hands to roll the rag up the wall in a straight, vertical column about 10cm (4in) wide. Use a plumb line as a guide for the first line. When the column is completed remove the rag.

5 Stop the columns where you can comfortably reach in one stretch, but stagger the tops. A wall can be split horizontally into three sections, so that each third can be done separately.

6 After about 1sq m (1sq yd), the rag will start to dry out. To wet the rag dip your hand into the solution and wipe it on the rag. Repeat once more. This will cover another area the same size.

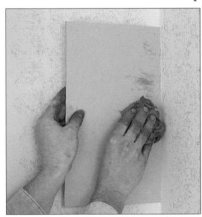

7 Use the ragging technique (see pages 44–45) in a vertical line at corners. Place the card strip against the adjacent wall to protect it as you work.

8 You can apply second and third colours over the first to create columns of mixed colour on top of each other, or stripes of colour side-by-side.

EFFECT OF ONE OR MORE COLOURS

Three colours create a luxurious blend

Ragging in a single cool colour

Ragging in a single warm colour

DESIGN IDEA
Rag rolling a wall produces a very sophisticated look, which can exploit the use of extra colours. Try it with three colours up to the dado rail, then use sponging or ragging on the wall above the dado.

Colour washing

Colour washing, with water-based paint solutions, can be used to produce finishes ranging from subtle clouding to a wild underwater shimmer. It does highlight a rough surface but this can be turned to advantage if you wish to create a distressed look.

TOOLS: Absorbent cloth, synthetic sponge

MATERIALS: Dust sheet, water-based paint solution, old plate

BASE: On walls colour wash over a base coat of water-based paint such as emulsion. On woodwork use a base of eggshell paint

COLOUR WASH TECHNIQUES

For walls choose from circular shapes, a random 'hay bundle' pattern or horizontal or vertical stripes.

Move the sponge over the surface in random circles or figures of eight. Create the hay-bundle pattern by swiping the surface in arcs of long, overlapping strokes. Make stripes with short overlapping strokes.

New wood absorbs the paint evenly. If the wood has been painted and stripped it is often difficult to get a consistent finish so make sure you do a test sample first. Varnish or wax-polish colour-washed furniture to protect it.

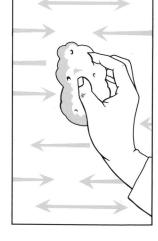

Circular shapes

Random patterns

Horizontal or vertical stripes

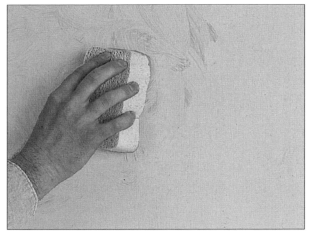

1 On a protected work surface, pour about 15 ml (1 tbsp) of paint solution (see pages 40–41) onto a plate and work it well into the sponge. Practice is very important before colour washing the chosen surface because both colour and pattern can vary so much. Try out the pattern (see opposite) and colour alternatives before you choose the colour and effect you prefer.

2 Using your chosen colour apply the sponge to the well-prepared and evenly painted wall, using the technique you have chosen. Work rapidly and re-wet the sponge when necessary. This is likely to be about every 1sq m (1sq yd). Use a small brush to get into awkward corners. Subsequent colours can be added, but it is best to allow one hour between coats for the paint to dry.

COLOUR–WASH EFFECTS ON WOOD AND PLASTER

◄ **One colour wash**
Choose a light or mid-tone background and wash in a slightly deeper tone. These orange shades blend for a warm and subtle effect.

► **Two colour wash**
Contrasting colours can be washed over each other.

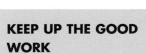

◄ **On new timber**
Colour washing emphasizes the grain and gives the wood a gently ageing look.

KEEP UP THE GOOD WORK
Work with speed when colour washing and try to maintain a wet edge. Always complete a wall in one go.

Protecting your work

Simple paint effects are very good at hiding lumps, bumps and scuff marks and do not usually need any protection to survive reasonable wear and tear on walls. Most water-based paints can be wiped clean, however certain areas which are specially prone to marks, such as hallways, kitchens and bathrooms, or furniture, fixtures and fittings, benefit from some form of protective finish.

If a gloss finish is used, any imperfections will be highlighted, while a matt or satin surface is a great deal more forgiving. However, some paint effects look wonderful coated with a full gloss varnish – colour washing in rich, dark colours is a good example.

TOOLS: Paintbrush, fine-grade sandpaper, fine-grade steel wool

MATERIALS: Varnish or other protective medium (see page 25)

▲ **MATT, SILK AND GLOSS FINISHES**
A matt finish leaves the colour unchanged, while silk and gloss finishes enrich and deepen the colour and create highlights.

◄ **OIL-BASED VARNISH**
This is available in matt, satin or gloss finish and may contain polyurethane which makes it very tough and heat-resistant. Oil-based varnishes all contain linseed oil and this has a slight yellowing effect which becomes stronger with time and which changes the tones of blues and reds. Use over oil glazes, especially if the item is subject to heavy wear. Brush on 2–3 coats and sand lightly between coats.

SPRAY VARNISH

This can be oil- or water-based. It is ideal for protecting small, ornate items (right). Use several thin coats rather that one thick one. Follow manufacturer's instructions when applying. Use fine steel wool to give a key between coats.

CAUTION

Carefully follow manufacturer's instructions and hazard warnings, especially when working with products that contain solvents. In general, work in a well-ventilated space, wear gloves and protective clothing and avoid skin contact.

ACRYLIC VARNISH

This is the best varnish for protecting water-based finishes which are exposed to wear, from furniture to boxes or a tea-tray. It comes in matt, satin or gloss. Apply with a brush or spray (for small objects). It has a milky colour while being applied, but dries clear. Use 2–3 coats and sand lightly before re-applying.

PROTECTIVE GLAZE

This is water-based and is very similar to acrylic varnish. Apply it by brush or spray, when it dries to provide an undetectable protective layer. However it is not as tough as some varnishes mentioned above.

Check the manufacturer's instructions to ensure compatability between the base and the protective medium.

CHANGING THE EFFECT

Include a protective finish when doing samples as a varnish may change the final effect.

More Advanced Paint Finishes

The flexibility provided by scumble glazes opens up opportunities for a whole new array of exciting effects. Scumble glazes, because they take some time to dry, allow much more time for work to be done on producing fine finishes and also allow more than one glaze to be blended and worked together on the surface at the same time. This produces effects that have a special depth and quality.

Neither acrylic nor oil glazes are tough finishes, and when used on surfaces such as doors, floors or furniture, they will need a coat of seal or varnish if they are to wear well. The material chosen must be compatible with the glaze used or you could damage your masterpiece. Whenever possible use the varnish recommended by the manufacturer of the glaze (see also pages 22–23 and 50–51).

This chapter contains

Mixing scumble glazes

Acrylic scumble glazes are non-toxic, non-yellowing, tough and water-based. They can be applied over vinyl silk emulsion, eggshell paint or melamine.

Oil scumble glaze is based on linseed oil, and gives high quality results, but it yellows with age and on exposure to high temperatures or to bright light. It can be used over eggshell or on top of a melamine base.

Acrylic scumble glaze
TOOLS: Small paintbrush or spoon

MATERIALS: Dust sheet, stencil paint, artists' acrylic paint or universal stainer, screw-top glass jar with rubber seal, acrylic scumble glaze, absorbent cloth

Oil scumble glaze
TOOLS: Small paintbrush or spoon

MATERIALS: Dust sheet, artists' oils, eggshell paint or universal stainer, transparent oil scumble glaze, screw-top glass jar with rubber seal, white spirit or turpentine, absorbent cloth

RELATIVE QUANTITIES OF COLOUR AND GLAZE TO SOLVENT

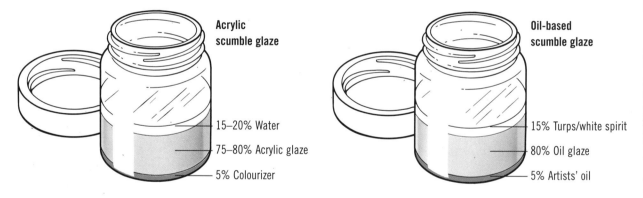

Acrylic scumble glaze
— 15–20% Water
— 75–80% Acrylic glaze
— 5% Colourizer

Oil-based scumble glaze
— 15% Turps/white spirit
— 80% Oil glaze
— 5% Artists' oil

USING GLAZES

	ACRYLIC SCUMBLE	OIL SCUMBLE
MAXIMUM WORKING TIME	30 minutes	90 minutes
DRYING TIME	2–4 hours	8–16 hours
COVERAGE	20–40 sq m per litre (12–25 sq yd per pint)	20–40 sq m per litre (12–25 sq yd per pint)
SUITABLE SURFACES	Vinyl silk emulsion Oil–based eggshell Melamine Varnished surfaces	Oil-based eggshell Melamine Varnished surfaces
SUITABLE COLOURANTS	Stencil or acrylic paints Universal stainer	Artists' oils, eggshell Universal stainer
COMMENTS	Water-based – dries clear	Easy to use but yellows with age

ACRYLIC SCUMBLE GLAZE

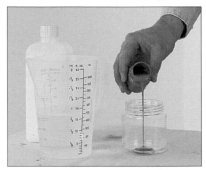  

1 Protect the working area and pour 15ml (1 tbsp) of the chosen paint, in this case stencil paint, into the jar. (If artists' acrylic is used a little water should be added and a brush or a spoon used to mix it.) Add water and scumble glaze, following the proportions shown left.

2 For a soft colour use about 1–part paint or stainer to 20–parts glaze, for a strong effect use about 1–part paint or stainer to 10–parts glaze. Replace the jar top, cover with a piece of old cloth, and shake vigorously.

3 Look at the jar base to check the paint is thoroughly mixed. If not, shake again.
Check the finished glaze for colour intensity and consistency by doing a sample. Wait for it to dry. If the colour is too strong or too pale, adjust and test again.

OIL-BASED SCUMBLE GLAZE

  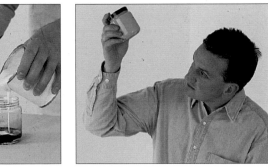

1 Protect the working area with the dust sheet. Squeeze about 5cm (2in) length of artists' oil paint into the re-sealable jar. Use a colour darker than the desired final colour. If you use eggshell paint or universal stainer use about 30ml (2 tbsp).

2 Add about 30ml (1fl oz) or 1cm (½in)-depth of white spirit or turpentine. Mix paint and solvent with a brush or spoon. Add about 150ml (5fl oz) or 5cm (2in) of scumble glaze. Don't use more than 20 per cent of solvent in the mixture so as not to over-thin the glaze. Seal the jar, cover and shake until creamy.

3 Check the base of the jar to see if there are any lumps in the mixture. Continue to shake the jar if the ingredients are not thoroughly mixed. This is very important because when using artists' oils, undissolved paint can create a glaze that changes colour as you work.

Dragging

Dragging is a subtle finish suitable for large areas such as walls, or for providing a soft, striped effect on doors, skirtings and panelling. Once the first colour is dry, subsequent colours can be applied to provide extra interest. Mixed-bristle dragging brushes give a more defined line, similar to combing (see pages 72–73).

TOOLS: 25mm (1in) size standard decorators' paint-brush, brush for dragging, (see box, page 57)

MATERIALS: Dust sheet, paint kettle, mixed glaze in one colour (see pages 54–55), old towel or absorbent cloth

BASE: This finish can be used over almost any plain-colour surface decorated in eggshell paint (see also pages 36–37))

1 Prepare the surface well first (see pages 32–37). Dragging tends to highlight any irregularities in the base. Protect the working area with the dust sheet and decant the glaze into a paint kettle.

2 Apply the mixed glaze using a standard decorators' brush. Spread it evenly over the surface.

3 Starting from a top corner, draw the dragging brush down through the glaze in vertical lines, holding it at an angle of approximately thirty degrees. Continue the stroke for as far as you can comfortably reach so that you avoid making too many joins.

4 If you want more defined lines apply greater pressure to the brush. Occasionally as you work, pull the dragging brush through the towel in order to keep it consistently dry.

5 A brush leaves a mark when first applied to a surface but no mark when taken off. To disguise joins in the dragging, work back over previous areas, starting from a bottom corner and dragging from the opposite direction. In this way only the corners will show brushmarks.

6 The result is a subtle grained effect, which highlights and enhances other decorations without overpowering them.

BRUSH UP ON YOUR EQUIPMENT

To ensure consistent results, slightly dampen your brush with glaze before starting work, since a damp brush creates a slightly different look to a dry one. If you don't have traditional dragging or flogging brushes you can use a long-bristled paintbrush, a dust brush, a distemper or wallpaper hanging brush instead.

Large areas of glaze can be applied quickly using a short-haired roller in place of a paint brush.

SHARP DRAGGED CORNERS

The frame of a panelled door is an ideal surface for a dragging technique.

First complete the horizontal rails, top and bottom, and then start vertical rails from the door edge, to create clean, sharp struck corners against the horizontal rails.

Rag rolling off

Rag rolling with glaze produces a depth and quality of finish which would be difficult to achieve in any other way. This variation on traditional rag rolling, which used only dry rags, should be compared with rag rolling on (see pages 46–47). There is no reason why the two techniques should not be combined to great advantage.

TOOLS: 25mm (1in) size standard decorators' paint-brush, pre-washed polyester and cotton or pure cotton rag about 30cm (12in) square

MATERIALS: Dust sheet, open-top tub, mixed glaze in one colour (see pages 54–55), thin rubber gloves, old towel or absorbent cloth

BASE: This finish can be used over a good-condition plain-colour surface decorated in eggshell paint (see also pages 36–37)

1 Cover the working area with the dust sheet. Transfer the mixed glaze (see pages 54–55) to the open-top tub, and immerse the rag in it.

2 Apply the mixed glaze evenly to the surface using the standard decorating brush. Finish off by painting in one direction only.

3 Wearing rubber gloves, remove the rag and wring it out. Take care to catch excess glaze in the tub and work into the rag any excess solution on your gloves.

4 Scrunch the rag into a sausage shape about 10cm (4in) long. Do not fold it as this creates an unattractive effect.

5 Apply the rag to the surface by gently rolling it upwards in a straight line, using both hands. When the first column is completed, overlap it slightly with the second to give a continuous finish.

6 It is easiest to complete walls in sections, taking the first section as high as you can comfortably reach and staggering the tops of the columns. A staggered top makes joints much easier to disguise.

7 As the cloth gets wetter the finish on the wall changes. To correct this, dab the rag on an absorbent cloth to dry it a little. Use a ragging technique (see pages 44–45) on constricted areas and corners.

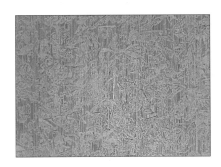

8 The result is ideal for a range of surfaces, from door panels to walls and even on floors.

ALTERNATIVE EFFECTS

Stippling
Stippling over the base glaze (left) then rag rolling gives a lightly textured effect (right).

Brushing
Brushing on the glaze randomly (left) then rag rolling off gives a crumpled effect (right).

THE MORE THE MERRIER

It is easier for two people to work together on large areas, one applying the glaze while the other does the ragging. Alternatively, use a short-haired roller to cover large areas quickly.

When doing a sample, check the effect a range of fabric rags can create, as you may prefer the finish of an alternative material. New fabrics should always be washed since the texture that they produce can change with use if not previously softened.

Stippling: one colour

Stippling is a way of creating shaded colour which has no obvious direction or texture. It looks very natural and forms a subtle backdrop. Use soft base colours such as white, cream or pastels, with stronger colour glazes over. Stippling can also be used in conjunction with other finishes, to reduce over-strong texture or unattractive brushmarks.

TOOLS: 25–75mm (1–3in) size standard decorators' paintbrush or short-haired roller (depending on size of area to be tackled), stippling and edge-stippling brushes

MATERIALS: Dust sheet, one mixed glaze (see pages 54–55), old towel or absorbent cloth

BASE: This finish can be used over a good-condition plain-colour surface decorated in eggshell paint (see also pages 36–37)

1 Using the standard decorators' paintbrush, apply the glaze randomly but evenly to the surface that is to be stippled. Alternatively, apply large areas of glaze using a short-haired roller.

2 Work a little glaze into the stippling brush to dampen it, then pound the surface, dabbing the brush evenly and firmly up and down and keeping it at right angles to the surface.

3 Control the density of the colour by removing glaze from the brush as it builds up. To do this dry the brush on the towel or absorbent cloth.

4 Continue to stipple the area, controlling the depth of colour by repeating step 3. Correct any mistakes immediately by stippling over them.

5 Use a narrow brush or edge-stippler to get a neat finish in awkward corners or against skirting boards or architrave.

6 The end result is a blend of background and glaze colours, with no obvious brushmarks, giving the surface a subtle, shaded effect.

Stippling: two colours

By developing this finish and using it to blend together two or more colours, you can create unusual shaded effects. This can produce subtle colour changes which can be used cleverly to change the apparent shape of a room (see box, page 63). A second colour can be used in defined areas or three areas of colour can subtly merge into each other.

TOOLS: 25mm (1in) size standard decorators' paintbrush, stippling and edge-stippling brushes

MATERIALS: Dust sheet, mixed glazes in two or more colours (see pages 54–55), old towel or absorbent cloth

BASE: This finish can be used over a good-condition and plain-colour surface decorated in eggshell paint (see also pages 36–37)

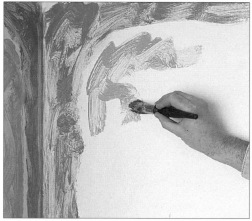

2 Using a second brush, apply the second-colour glaze in the same random way to the area to be covered by this colour.

1 Using the standard decorators' brush apply the first of the glazes randomly but evenly over the area to be covered by that colour.

3 Work a little of the first glaze into the stippling brush to dampen it and pound the glaze keeping the brush at right angles (see step 2, page 60).

4 Once the first colour has been stippled, roughly clean the stippling brush on the old towel or take a second, clean brush ready to stipple the second colour. Some blending and mixing of the two colours is inevitable and desirable.

5 Pound the second colour with the clean stippling brush, until you are happy with the texture created. Correct mistakes as they happen, by simply stippling over them.

6 Where colours meet, slowly blend the edges, merging the colours until the desired mix is achieved. The density of colour and texture can be controlled by drying the brush regularly on the absorbent cloth.

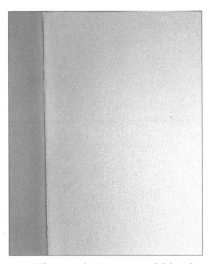

7 Tidy up the corners and edges using a narrow brush or the narrow edge-stippler. It may be necessary to dry the brush frequently to remove excess glaze from the corners.

8 The result is a natural blend of colours which can be used with great effect on almost any surface, large or small.

THINK SMALL
Use a stencil brush to stipple small items.

TRICKS WITH COLOUR
If one colour is used, with a second colour on the central areas, the stippling softens the edges and wall corners and gives an impression of age.

Applying three tones of one colour in lightly merging horizontal stripes, dark at the bottom and light at the top, makes the wall appear higher than it really is.

Bagging: one colour

Bagging proves how easy paint finishing can be. There are few things cheaper and more widely available than plastic bags which, when scrunched up, produce swirling shapes and patterns. You can also experiment with this technique with other objects. Try out a range of simple everyday household items to find out what patterns and unusual decorative finishes they create.

TOOLS: 25mm (1in) size standard decorators' paint-brush, plastic carrier bag

MATERIALS: Dust sheet, mixed glaze in one colour (see pages 54–55), old towel or absorbent cloth

BASE: This finish can be used over a plain-colour surface decorated in eggshell (see also pages 36–37)

1 Using the standard decorators' brush, apply the glaze randomly but evenly to the surface.

2 Turn the plastic bag inside out, then scrunch it up to form a shape that is comfortable to hold.

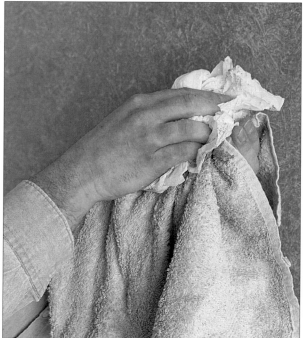

3 Gently pat the surface with the bag, reforming the bag shape periodically to create new patterns. Work with speed, paying particular attention to corners, and aim for an even finish.

4 Glaze can be removed from the bag by occasionally drying it with a towel. Clean more regularly if you want a finer texture and a softer colour.

5 The resulting pattern is dappled and grainy and looks rather like an exotic polished stone. It is important to maintain a wet glaze while working on it but, because this is a fast technique, even large areas can be covered by one person.

PLASTIC ARTS
Experiment with different qualities and thicknesses of bags to create a whole range of textures. Before using it, turn the bag inside out, as the printing on the outside dissolves when using glaze and could therefore spoil the look of your work.

Bagging: two colours

Two-colour bagging is a remarkably easy way to blend two colours together to create a fascinating texture. Apart from being effective on its own, two-colour bagging can provide the ideal background for marbling (see pages 86–87). It is quick to do and could not be easier or cheaper to achieve.

TOOLS: Two 25mm (1in) size standard decorators' paintbrushes, plastic carrier bags

MATERIALS: Dust sheet, mixed glazes in two colours (see pages 54–55), absorbent cloth or old towel

BASE: This finish can be used over a plain-colour surface decorated in eggshell (see also pages 36–37). It is effective for walls, furniture and fittings from door panels to table tops

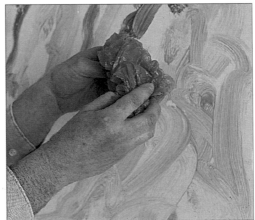

2 Turn your bag inside out and scrunch it up into a controllable shape. Bag size, thickness and the way it is held all play their part.

1 Using the two standard decorators' brushes, one for each colour, apply both glazes randomly but evenly over the same area of surface but not on top of each other. To achieve a marbled effect, as here, work over a pale ivory base coat. The main glaze is in a mid-tone yellow, and smaller areas of a darker brown glaze – sparingly applied – subtly suggest the strands and fissures in the stone.

3 Dab the bag over the surface (see step 3, page 65), applying it to one colour first. Continue to work on the area until a reasonable texture is achieved.

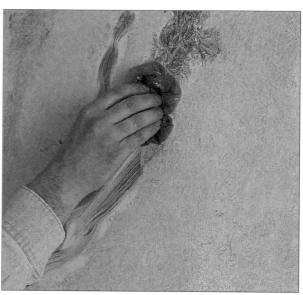

4 Clean the bag, using the towel, ready for applying it to the second colour areas. Alternatively replace the bag with a new one.

5 Dab the bag over the second colour (repeating step 3, opposite). Some overlap and mixing of colour is inevitable and desirable at this stage.

FANTASY MARBLE
Use this technique to create a fantasy marble effect for hall walls or for a dining room in the area below a dado rail.

6 Now carefully blend the colours by working from one glaze to the other. Continue until you achieve a look you are happy with. Glaze can be removed, and the texture changed, by drying the bag with the towel.

7 The blended and textured result is both quick and easy to achieve. It appears intriguing and looks difficult to produce. This just goes to prove how looks can be deceiving!

Colour washing

A colour wash using glaze creates a layer of colour through which the background colour can still be seen. A range of effects can be achieved using a brush or sponge. A brush gives a bolder, uneven finish where streaks appear and the base colour shows through more strongly in some places than others. A sponge creates a subtle haze. Do a sample before you start, to enable you to try a variety of effects and choose the most suitable.

Using brushes
TOOLS: 25mm (1in) size standard decorators' paint-brush or short-haired roller, dragging brush or flogger

MATERIALS: Dust sheet, mixed glaze in one colour (see pages 54–55), old towel or absorbent cloth

Using a sponge
TOOLS: Synthetic sponge

MATERIALS: Dust sheet, mixed glaze in one colour (see pages 54–55), old plate, absorbent cloth or old towel

BASE: This finish can be used over a plain-colour surface decorated in eggshell (see also pages 36–37)

USING BRUSHES

1 Apply the glaze randomly but evenly to the surface using a standard decorators' brush. As it is important to maintain a wet working edge, on large areas you may require two people. Alternatively use a short-haired roller to apply the glaze quickly.

2 Use a dragging brush, first dampened in the glaze, and make short, random strokes, building up the pattern chosen from your sample. Larger areas can be covered with a wider flogging brush. Dry the brush with a towel to remove glaze and to create a more subtle colour.

3 The result is a three-dimensional, luminous finish that is equally suitable for walls, floors, furniture or even china. Subsequent colours can be added if required once the previous layer is completely dry.

USING A SPONGE

1 Prepare a protected working area and assemble all your materials. Pour a little glaze onto the plate and mop up with the synthetic sponge. Work the sponge around the plate and check that the glaze is evenly distributed throughout the sponge.

2 Use the sponge to spread the glaze over the surface in random swirls. Re-apply more glaze to the sponge whenever this is necessary.

3 The result is a distinctive and very individual effect. This can be enhanced by the addition of further colours once the original coat has dried.

TWO-COLOUR VARIATIONS

Swirls
Swirls, using two colours of a similar tone, create this delicate effect. Allow the first coat to dry completely, then repeat the process with the second colour.

Swiping
Swiping the surface with widely sweeping brushstrokes in first one colour, then a second when the first is dry, creates a bolder and more uneven texture.

BRUSH EFFECTS
Random, over-lapping brushstrokes gradually build up over the surface, giving the result shown opposite, but a checkerboard, tartan or sheaf of hay finish can all be achieved too.

SPONGE EFFECTS
Random, circular and sweeping strokes made with a sponge give a cloud-like appearance.

Colour rubbing off

This is a technique which highlights the patterns in an embossed surface.
A glaze in a darker colour is applied over a light-colour base. The raised areas of the design are rubbed to expose the base colour while the top-colour glaze appears more strongly in relief areas. This emphasizes the three-dimensional nature of the surface. However, test a small area first, as rubbing can show up seams in embossed paper.

Embossed wall coverings
TOOLS: 50mm (2in) size standard decorators' paint-brush or short-haired roller rubber-bladed window-cleaning squeegee

MATERIALS: Dust sheet, mixed glaze in one colour (see pages 54–55), old towel

Plasterwork and carvings
TOOLS: Two 50mm (2in) size standard decorators' paint-brushes, rubber-bladed window-cleaning squeegee

MATERIALS: Dust sheet, mixed glazes in two colours (see pages 54–55), absorbent, lint-free cloth

BASE: Use eggshell paint (see pages 36–37)

EMBOSSED WALL COVERINGS

1 Use darker glazes over a light-colour eggshell paint base (see also pages 36–37).

2 Apply the glaze evenly to the embossed surface using a standard decorators' brush or short-haired roller.

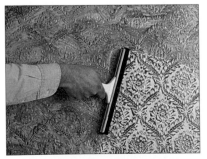

3 Gently wipe over the surface with the squeegee, working in all directions to ensure an even finish.

4 Remove excess glaze from the squeegee when it builds up, using the old towel. Continue to work over the whole surface.

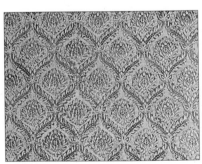

5 The result is a build-up of glaze in the crevices, and little on the areas of high relief, so exposing the pattern of the design.

PLASTERWORK AND CARVINGS

1 Apply two colour glazes randomly but evenly to the surface using standard decorators' brushes. Blue and brown blend to produce an 'aged' effect.

2 Use the brush in an up-and-down stippling action (see pages 62–63), until the colours partially blend.

3 Form a pad from the absorbent, lint-free cloth, and wipe this carefully over the surface. Turn and reform the cloth as it becomes covered in glaze to provide a constantly clean pad.

4 The result has the look of a patina produced by age, with an appealing blend of colours. Additional colour or a crackle finish (see pages 80–81) can be added once this base is thoroughly dry.

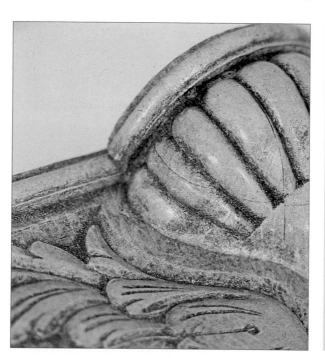

VARIATIONS

For large areas of shallow moulding a short-haired roller could be used to distribute the glaze in step 1.

A ragged texture can be achieved by using a scrunched up rag to dab the surface when step 3 has been completed. Experiment with household materials for different finishes.

Combing

Combing was originally designed to give a simple wood grain effect. In fact, it is much more versatile than this. Combs can be used to create a wide range of patterns from simple trellis or cane effects to wild or delicate three-dimensional moiré patterns, even impressive tartans.

TOOLS: 25mm (1in) size standard decorators' paint-brush or short-haired roller, stippling brush, comb

MATERIALS: Dust sheet, mixed glaze in one colour (see pages 54–55), old towel or absorbent cloth

BASE: This finish can be used over a plain-colour surface decorated in eggshell (see also pages 36–37)

1 Apply the glaze evenly to the surface using the decorators' brush. To cover large areas quickly use a short-haired roller or alternatively seek the help of a partner or friend.

2 Stipple the surface (see pages 60–61) to remove brushstrokes and ensure even distribution of the glaze. When necessary, remove glaze from the brush with the towel.

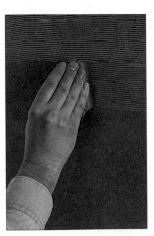

3 Hold the comb at approximately thirty degrees to the surface, and draw it through the glaze. Different finishes can be achieved by varying the pressure and the angle.

4 Remove excess glaze regularly by cleaning the comb with the towel. If you are not happy with the finish repeat steps 2–4.

COMBING PATTERNS

Moiré
Straight, overlapping, slanted lines interact to create a moiré effect.

Basket
A simple basket weave looks good used in panels with a dragged surround (see pages 56–57).

Swirls
Try your hand at freehand drawing, using a comb like a calligraphy pen.

Music
The theme shown here would appeal to a budding musician.

MAKE YOUR OWN COMBS
You can make your own combs by cutting them out from a piece of stiff card or a rubber window-cleaning squeegee.

Antiquing and Illusions

In time the finish on old furniture and decorative items crazes, fades and wears and these signs of age are what antiquing seeks to copy. Antiquing techniques cleverly use the interaction between incompatible materials to mimic age very successfully. Look carefully at old, worn surfaces to see where ageing occurs naturally – usually on corners, edges and around handles – then use this information to create a reliable copy.

Paint effects can also be used to mimic expensive materials like marble or to reproduce wood grains. These illusionary techniques are best included where the materials they copy would naturally appear in the home. Wherever possible use a sample of the real thing as a guide to colours and patterns.

Distressing

Distressing produces a worn, country look on new furniture or panelling. It is achieved by removing part of the top coat of paint to display a different colour base and by using metal objects such as keys and chains to bruise the surface and mimic wear. Although water-based paint is used here, you can also create the finish with oil-based paints.

TOOLS: 50mm (2in) size or a range of standard decorators' paintbrushes, keys on a ring or metal chain, steel wool, fine-grade sandpaper

MATERIALS: Emulsion paints in two contrasting colours, petroleum jelly

BASE: This finish can be used over a natural wood surface (see also pages 36–37). Use it to decorate furniture, wall panels, skirtings, doors and other woodwork

1 Using the standard decorators' brush and the colour which is to show through the distressed areas, paint on the base coat. Once this is dry, apply small smears of petroleum jelly with your thumb to the areas which you want to show through the top surface. Pay special attention to corners and along the edges.

2 Old furniture shows its age in the knocks and bruises associated with everyday life. If you want to mimic this on a brand new piece of furniture, use a bunch of keys or a chain and beat against the surface to bruise it and make it look 'worn'.

3 Once you are happy with the worn effect of the surface, apply the top coat of paint over the whole surface in the normal way and leave to dry.

4 Take the steel wool, form it into a pad, and rub it over the surface vigorously. The top coat does not adhere to areas covered with the petroleum jelly, so paint is easily removed here.

5 If you need to soften the edges and remove additional paint, smooth with fine-grade sandpaper to display more of the colour applied earlier.

6 Over water-based paint, or if the surface is scratched, apply two to three coats of varnish, sanding lightly between coats to provide a key. This will ensure that the surface can withstand further unwanted abuse.

7 The result is a worn, two-colour surface that would blend well with old furniture and furnishings.

ADDING COLOURS

If you prefer, more than one colour may be used to copy layers of paint built up over the years.

For additional highlights rub a little gilding cream over the surface at the end.

DECORATORS' TIPS

You can use a wax candle in place of petroleum jelly. Just rub the tip of the candle over the areas where you don't want the paint to adhere.

Water-based Buttermilk emulsion or Shaker paints produce the soft and subtle colours associated with age.

Choose colours that contrast, so that one shows up against the other. Both colours should blend well with your decorating scheme.

Wax ageing

This effect relies upon the interaction between turpentine-based wax and water-based emulsion to produce an overall faded look. This finish is similar to, but a little more subtle than, the distressing on pages 76–77, where wear areas are clearly defined. The wax, applied with wire wool, softens the paint and allows areas of top-coat paint to be easily removed.

TOOLS: 25mm (1in) size standard decorators' paint-brush, medium to fine-grade steel wool

MATERIALS: Dust sheet, matt emulsion paint in two contrasting colours, turpentine-based furniture wax, clean, soft cloth

BASE: This finish is best used on small or ornate objects, such as picture frames, and turned wood such as banister and towel rails, as shown here. Prepare the surface (see also pages 36–37)

WAX DISTRESSING

1 Protect your working area with the dust sheet. Prepare the item to be finished (see pages 34–35), then apply one coat of matt emulsion using the standard decorators' brush. Leave to dry.

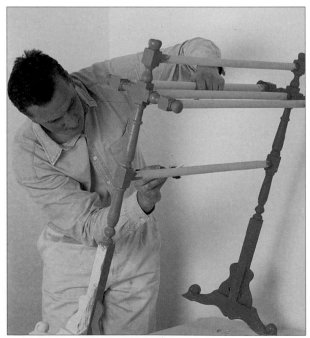

2 Once the first coat is dry, apply the contrasting colour emulsion paint and leave this to dry thoroughly as well.

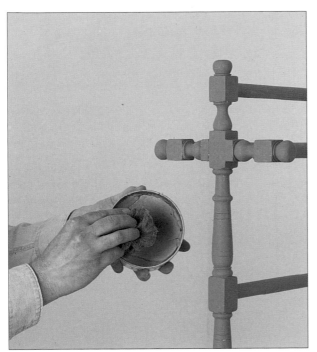

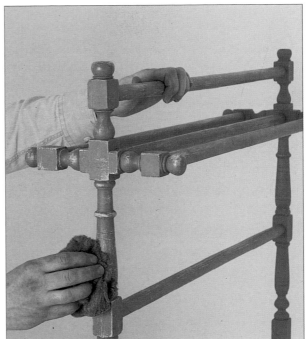

3 Form the steel wool into a pad and work a little wax into it. Vigorously rub the pad all over the decorated surface.

4 Aim to remove only a part of the emulsion top coat over the complete surface. Continue until you feel enough of the top coat has been removed, then leave the wax to harden.

5 Once the wax is hard, buff it up to a satin sheen using a soft cloth. This easily produced distressed finish is cleverly misleading and surprisingly durable.

SMALL IS BEAUTIFUL
A small amount of artists' oil paint can applied with the steel wool and wax (see steps 3 and 4) to enhance the finish.

Acrylic crackle finishes

Acrylic crackle glaze and varnish produce fascinating crazed surfaces which make new objects, such as shelves or boxes, look like old prized pieces. Crackle glaze works by splitting two layers of water-based paint so that the first coat shows through the cracks. Crackle varnish creates a webbing of fine cracks over a base coat.

Acrylic crackle glaze
TOOLS: 25mm (1in) size standard decorators' paint-brush, fine-grade steel wool, fine-grade sandpaper

MATERIALS: Dust sheet, matt emulsion or acrylic paint in two colours, acrylic crackle glaze, fine-grade sandpaper, matt acrylic varnish

Acrylic crackle varnish
TOOLS: As crackle glaze

MATERIALS: Dust sheet, emulsion or acrylic paint, crackle varnish and crackle glaze, clean, soft cloth, artists' oil paint, white spirit, matt acrylic varnish

BASE: Use over acrylic paints or emulsion and prepare the surface well (see pages 34–35)

ACRYLIC CRACKLE GLAZE

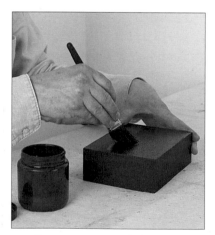

1 Protect your working area with the dust sheet. Use the standard decorators' brush to paint your chosen item in matt emulsion or acrylic paint using the colour which you wish to show through the cracks.

2 Once this base coat has thoroughly dried, apply an even coat of acrylic crackle glaze, brushing it on in one direction only. Apply the thickness decided on by doing some test samples (see Testing Crackle Glaze box opposite). Leave to dry.

3 Next, apply the top-coat colour, using a well-loaded brush and steady strokes, and working in the same direction as for the crackle glaze. Avoid going over the surface more than once with the brush, as cracks start to form immediately.

4 Leave the surface to dry. You will find cracks will continue to form as the top coat dries, revealing the base paint colour beneath.

5 When the object is dry, sand it lightly and brush on one coat of matt acrylic varnish to protect the finish.

ACRYLIC CRACKLE VARNISH

1 Apply a base coat of emulsion or acrylic paint in your chosen colour. When this is dry, use the standard decorators' brush to apply a sealing mixture of crackle glaze and crackle varnish in equal proportions.

2 Once this sealer layer has thoroughly dried, apply an even but thin layer of acrylic crackle varnish, brushing it on in one direction only. As this thin layer dries, it shrinks to create a web of fine surface cracks.

3 To highlight these cracks, rub a little artists' oil paint over the surface when dry using a soft cloth. Remove any excess paint with a cloth dampened in white spirit.

4 Leave the work to dry, then varnish to protect it.

HIGHLIGHTING

With crackle glaze, colours of similar intensity produce the best results. Try using gilding cream, in place of artists' oils, to add glitter to the cracks.

TESTING CRACKLE GLAZE

The thickness of the coat of glaze determines the end result – the thicker it is, the more marked the result – and therefore it is wise to do samples first to ensure you get the final effect you are aiming for.

Craquelure

Craquelure creates a more delicate crazed effect than the crackle finishes described on pages 80–81, so it is ideal for use over fine decoration such as decoupage, stencilling and hand-painted finishes. The craquelure is transparent and gives a delicate suggestion of age.

TOOLS: 25mm (1in) size decorators' paintbrushes, hair dryer
MATERIALS: Dust sheet, acrylic or oil-based varnish (step 1), patina varnish, cracking varnish, artists' oil paints, soft rags, white spirit or turpentine, oil-based varnish (step 5)

BASE: Use craquelure to age delicate decoration such as decoupage, stencilling and hand-painted finishes. Prepare the surface as described in step 1 below

1 Protect the working area with the dust sheet. Brush on acrylic- or oil-based varnish over the previously painted surface to seal it completely. Allow to dry thoroughly. Once dry, apply a coat of patina varnish as evenly as possible.

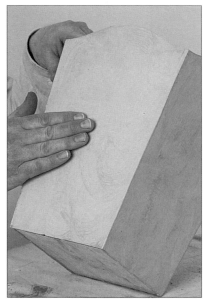

2 Humidity, air flow and temperature all affect the drying rate, but the surface should be left only until it is tacky or just touch dry. As a general rule, the drier the base coat, the finer the resulting cracks will be.

3 Immediately the surface is ready (see step 2), apply an even coat of gum arabic (cracking varnish) over the base coat. If the cracking varnish tends to split and separate, mix a little household detergent with it to help to reduce this. Leave to dry.

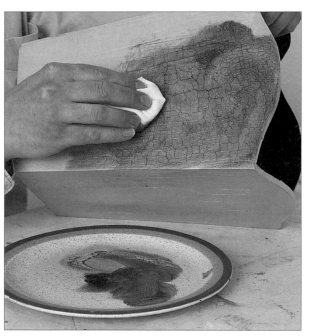

4 Use a hair dryer on a low heat to speed up the drying process of the varnish. Fast drying tends to create larger cracks than would otherwise occur.

5 Once the surface is thoroughly dry, highlight the cracks by rubbing artists' oil paint into them, using a soft rag. Remove any excess paint with a little white spirit or turpentine. When the artists' oil paint has dried, varnish the surface using oil-based varnish.

6 The result is a crazed finish which looks surprisingly natural. Both plain and decorated items can be enhanced using this technique.

SURFACE HIGHLIGHTS
Water-based highlighting mediums must not be used, as water will soften the cracking varnish. If you want to give the surface a metallic gleam use gilding cream rubbed into the cracks.

Liming

Traditional liming goes back to the 16th century when lime was used to keep woodworm at bay. This lethal material has now been replaced with a much safer alternative that adds the same whitish gleam and highlights the grain of the wood.

TOOLS: Stiff wire brush, fine-grade steel wool

MATERIALS: Dust sheet, liming paste, furniture wax, soft cloth or brush

BASE: Stripped or bare wood forms the best base. On painted or varnished wood prepare the surface by thoroughly stripping it using a proprietary stripper

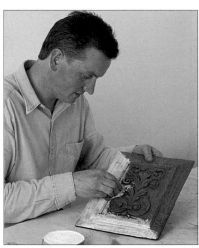

2 Using fine-grade steel wool, work a little liming paste into the surface of the wood, rubbing in all directions.

1 Protect the work area with a dust sheet. Brush the stripped or bare wood surface vigorously with the stiff brass brush to remove soft grain and create a roughened surface.

3 Leave the item until the paste has practically dried (a cool place is best). When ready, work a small amount of furniture wax into a clean ball of steel wool.

4 Rub the wax over the limed surface in circular movements. Turn the steel wool frequently and re-apply wax to it when necessary.

5 Once the desired finish is achieved leave for approximately 30 minutes, then buff up the surface to a satin finish, using a soft cloth or brush.

6 The liming paste gives a traditional whitish sheen to a clearly defined grained surface.

CAUTION
Always read the manufacturer's instructions and hazard warnings carefully when using paint stripper.

IT'S A WHITEWASH
A white colour wash (see pages 48–49) applied to untreated bare wood, and then rubbed down with steel wool and wax when dry is a good alternative to liming.

Basic marbling

Marbling is an art form in its own right, but more than adequate results can be achieved quickly and easily. You will obtain a much more realistic effect if you copy a piece of real marble or use a photograph of marble as a reference. It is best to start on a small area, such as a shelf or coffee table.

TOOLS: Plastic bags, old plate, natural sea sponge, stippling brush, feathers, fine artists' brush, softening brush

MATERIALS: Glazes in two or more colours, white spirit or turpentine, artists' oil paint

BASE: This finish can be used over a plain-colour surface decorated in eggshell paint (see also pages 36–37). Marbling is ideal for use on items that might naturally be made of marble, such as table tops, shelves and lamp bases

1 Use the bagging technique (see pages 66–67) to blend two or more coloured glazes together over the surface. Pour a small amount of white spirit or turpentine onto an old plate. Mop this up with a natural sea sponge and lightly dab all over the glazed surface.

2 After a minute or so the surface breaks up into small, fossil-like patterns. If none appear the glaze is too dry, in which case remove all the glaze using a lint-free cloth and solvent and start again. Remove excess solvent before proceeding by lightly stippling the surface or dabbing it with a soft, absorbent cloth.

3 Use artists' oils, thinned slightly with a little solvent or glaze mixture, to paint veins. A fine artists' brush is suitable, but experiment with other fine brushes. The aim is to achieve a natural vein copy, so check the patterns of veins as they appear on your example.

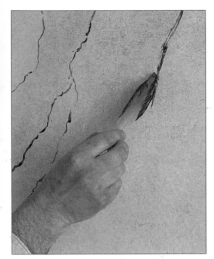

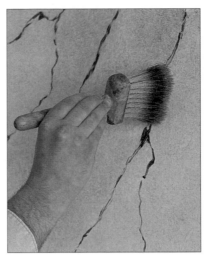

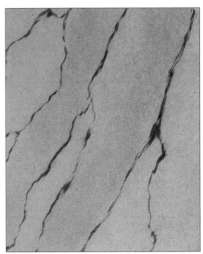

4 The edge of a feather, close to the tip, creates a natural vein effect but using it needs practice. Veins should all run in one direction and continue over the edge of a surface. Be careful not to over-vein.

5 Use a softening brush to soften the hard lines of the veins. Manipulate the brush with very light pendulum strokes. First work in the direction of the veins and then at right angles to them. If brush-strokes appear, you are being too heavy-handed so make movements lighter.

6 The result is a blended and textured background with veins running through it. Once this surface has dried completely, additional layers of glaze can be added to enhance the final result.

ALTERNATIVE METHOD

If you do not want to soften the background as in step 5 you can leave the bagged surface to dry and apply the veins later.

A clean dusting or dragging brush is a good alternative to a softener.

Additional layers of glaze and veining help to enhance the finish and create the depth of colour and texture found in natural marble.

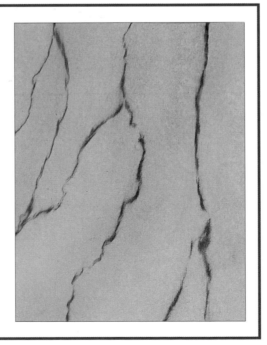

SPLATTER TECHNIQUE

White spirit can be splattered over the wet, glazed surface using a short-bristled brush, such as a stencil brush. Tap the shaft of the brush on a ruler or the side of your hand to obtain the necessary shower of tiny specks of white spirit.

Marbling a large area

Most natural stone, including marble, is cut and used as slabs. Therefore, if you want large areas of marbling to look authentic, you need to break them down into smaller blocks for decorating. Slab shapes can be drawn up to represent individual blocks, and even intricate mosaic patterns can be created. Careful advance work is essential. Draw up a layout, to scale, and mark in the slab positions on this, then use your plan to draw up the design on the area to be decorated. Realistic patterns and shapes not only enhance the effect but make the marbling easier to complete.

TOOLS: Metal rule, straight edge, pencil or chalk, masking tape, lining pen

BASE: This finish can be used over a plain-colour surface decorated in eggshell paint (see also pages 36–37). This method is ideal for use on floors, walls and work surfaces

PLANNING LARGE AREAS

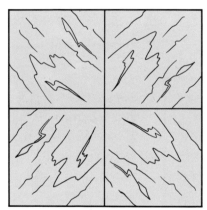

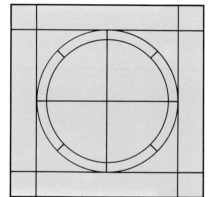

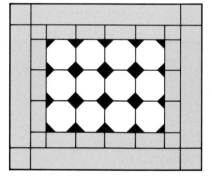

1 For an over-all fantasy effect, marbling can cover large areas in one continuous sweep. However, for a realistic effect you need to create the appearance of slabs of marble. The pattern should radiate from a central point and should consist of mirror images.

2 Areas can also be broken into more complex arrangements. You will need to measure the surface area carefully and draw up a plan to scale. Then work out your design on this plan.

3 Once you are happy with the design, transfer it to the area to be marbled. Use a steel rule to measure distances accurately and use chalk or a soft pencil and a straight edge to draw out the design carefully.

4 You need to allow one slab area to dry before tackling those adjacent to it. Devise an order of work and number squares accordingly to avoid any problem. Use masking tape to protect adjacent squares while you work on one, then move to an area that does not touch the wet slab and allow sufficient drying time before tackling adjacent shapes.

5 Fantasy marble may be created covering large areas. For a more realistic look use a soft pencil and straight edge to mark the joints between blocks. Finally, varnish the surface to protect it. This is particularly important in areas such as halls and stairways which get heavy wear.

SOFTENED EFFECTS

Marbling techniques can be used in soft shades and an impressionistic manner to create a restful impression that is easy to live with.

WORKING VEINING

Take your time over veining and work on one panel at a time only. Don't over-vein. In marble veins are never parallel, wobbly or cobweb-like, nor do they break but they may split and form junctions.

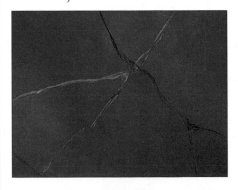

Wood graining

Wood graining can be used to imitate natural wood, or to create wood patterns in unnatural colours. Plywood and medium density fibreboard can be enhanced with expensive hardwood grains. Here a comb is used for one finish, and a rocker for the other. The rocker has a curved and embossed face and is used in a gentle rocking motion, changing the angle of the face. Do some samples first, so that you are confident of your technique before you start on the area to be decorated.

Using a comb
TOOLS: 25mm (1in) size standard decorators' paint-brush, softening brush, comb (metal or rubber)

MATERIALS: Dust sheet, mixed glaze in one colour (see pages 54–55), absorbent cloth

BASE: A plain-colour wood surface decorated in eggshell paint (see also pages 36–37).

Using a rocker
TOOLS: 25mm (1in) size standard decorators' paint-brush, straight edge, rocker

MATERIALS: Dust sheet, mixed glaze in one colour (see pages 54–55), varnish, absorbent cloth

BASE: This finish can be used over a plain-colour surface decorated in egg-shell paint (see also pages 36–37).

USING A COMB

1 Brush on the glaze in random arcs. Then repeatedly pull the comb through the glaze, cleaning it on the cloth after each stroke.

2 Use a softening brush, with steady, light strokes, to feather and soften the hard edges.

3 Wrap an absorbent rag around your forefinger and wipe through the glaze in random arcs. Comb through the glaze.

4 Use the softening brush to soften hard edges until the desired effect is achieved. Protect with varnish when dry.

USING A ROCKER

1 Apply the glaze evenly to the surface using the decorators' brush. Follow the direction of the grain with the brushstrokes.

2 To mimic boarding, place a straight edge against the surface. Steadily draw the rocker through the glaze, guided by the straight edge, gently rocking it back and forth.

3 Move the straight edge over and lay it parallel with the previous line, forming a gap which is slightly greater than the width of the rocker. Repeat the rest of step 2.

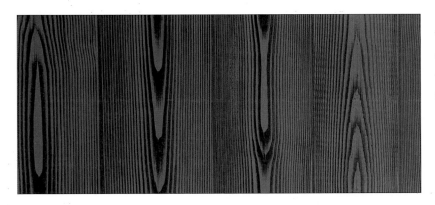

4 The result shows a realistic and easily achieved pine woodgrain. Once the glaze is dry, varnish the surface to protect and enhance it.

COLOURFUL EFFECTS

Do not be afraid to use bright colours for this effect. These samples illustrate the effect using strong colours and overlapping the strokes of the rocker.

SMOOTH ROCKING

Pre-tinted oil scumbles, in assorted wood colours, are available from specialist suppliers. Wipe a little lubricant, such as silicon, onto the straight edge to help to smooth the rocking process.

Glossary

Acrylic
A fast drying water-based material, drying to a tough waterproof finish.

Ageing
The process of simulating the effect of age through natural wear.

Artists' oils
Oil-borne pigment ideal for tinting transparent oil glaze.

Badger brush
A high quality, expensive softening brush for use with advanced glaze finishes (see page 20 for alternatives).

Bagging
A paint finish utilizing plastic bags.

Beeswax
High quality wax polish.

Cissing
The splitting of the top layer of paint causing globules or channels.

Colour rubbing
The removal of glaze from certain areas using a cloth.

Colour washing
A general description of a subtle colour effect created using sponges or brushes.

Complementary colours
Two colours which enliven each other.

Crackle glaze
A medium which induces splitting or cracking when used between two layers of water-based paints.

Craquelure
Fine quality crazing created by using two varnishes which work against each other.

Distressing
Imitating wear and tear on painted surfaces (see Ageing).

Dragging
Creating a lined contrast effect using glaze.

Eggshell
A durable oil-based, mid-sheen paint which is an ideal base for most glaze finishes.

Emulsion
A water-based paint ideal for most types of wall decoration.

Emulsion glaze
A water-based latex which creates a clear protective seal for the paint effect.

Flogger
Long mixed bristle brush for wood graining or dragging.

Glaze
A transparent medium which may be tinted to any colour and used for paint effects.

Graining
Imitating true wood grain using glazes.

Liming
Adding a white highlight and finish to an open grain timber.

Linseed oil
The base for traditional oil-based paints and transparent oil glaze.

Marbling
Imitating true stone.

Melamine
Plastic spray coating which may be paint finished.

Pigment
Natural colour source.

Primary colours
Yellow, blue and red, from which all other colours may be mixed.

Ragging
Use of a rag to create a decorative paint effect.

Rocker
A tool used to imitate wood grain.

Sandpaper
Abradsive sheet for removing roughness.

Scumble
Another term for glaze.

Softener
Brush for smoothing and toning effects to create a natural look.

Solvent
A cleaning or thinning medium for paint.

Universal stainers
A pigment-bearing medium suitable for tinting paints and glazes.

Varnish
A protective medium which may be water- or oil-based.

Index

*The authors and publishers would like to thank the
following for their assistance in producing this book:*

Janice Frost and family, Jenny Martin, Marina Tzirka and the Greek Orthodox Church,
Stephanie and Kavan Hashemi Brown, The Allen Brothers of Birmingham,
James and Sandra Crow, Sue Cassels, Jackie Steadman, Alison and Mark Rowley,
Mrs Piper, Bill and Lorraine Graham, Jackie Gilbert

Jessica Earle

All the staff in our shops who have borne the extra burden
while we have been working on this book

For mail order and sales information contact: The Painted Finish, Unit 6,
Hatton Country World, Hatton, Warwick, England CV35 8XA

Editor: Jenny Plucknett
Sub-editor: Margaret Crowther
Designers: Pedro Prá-Lopez and
Frances Prá-Lopez,
(Kingfisher Design)
Frank Landamore

Managing Editor: Miranda Spicer
Art Director: Martin Lovelock

Photography and styling: Debi Treloar

Illustrator: Fred van Deelen

Production Manager: Kevin Perrett
Set Builder: Nigel Tate

Peter Knott and Paula Knott have asserted their
right to be identified as the authors of this work.

First published 1996
Reprinted 1997, 1998, 1999

Text, photographs and illustrations
© Haynes Publishing 1996

Published by: Haynes Publishing
Sparkford, Nr Yeovil, Somerset BA22 7JJ

British Library Cataloguing-in-Publication Data:
A catalogue record for this book is available from
the British Library

ISBN 1 85960 109 X

Printed in France by
Imprimerie Pollina, 85400 Luçon - n° 77471